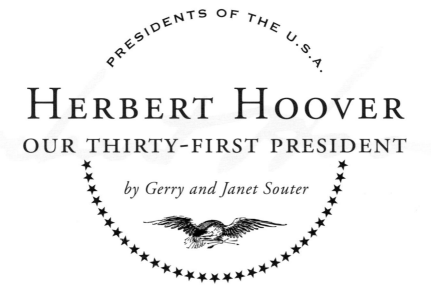

PRESIDENTS OF THE U.S.A.

HERBERT HOOVER
OUR THIRTY-FIRST PRESIDENT

by Gerry and Janet Souter

THE CHILD'S WORLD®

PUBLISHED IN THE UNITED STATES OF AMERICA

THE CHILD'S WORLD®
1980 Lookout Drive • Mankato, MN 56003-1705
800-599-READ • www.childsworld.com

ACKNOWLEDGMENTS
The Child's World®: Mary Berendes, Publishing Director

Creative Spark: Mary McGavic, Project Director; Melissa McDaniel, Editorial
Director; Deborah Goodsite, Photo Research

The Design Lab: Kathleen Petelinsek, Design; Gregory Lindholm, Page Production

Content Adviser: David R. Smith, Adjunct Assistant Professor of History,
University of Michigan–Ann Arbor

PHOTOS
Cover and page 3: White House Historical Association (White House Collection),
(detail); White House Historical Association (White House Collection)

Interior: Alamy: 7 (Robert Harding Picture Library Ltd.), 16 (The Print
Collector); Associated Press Images: 5 and 38, 10, 11 and 38, 25, 27, 37;
Corbis: 9, 13, 14, 31 (Corbis), 15, 21, 35, 36 (Bettmann), 20 (Hulton-Deutsch
Collection), 22 (Swim Ink 2, LLC), 33 (PEMCO—Webster & Stevens Collection;
Museum of History and Industry, Seattle); Getty Images: 23 (Hulton Archive),
32 (MPI), 24 and 39 (Popperfoto); The Herbert Hoover Presidential Library and
Museum: 4, 8, 12, 18, 19; The Image Works: 28, 34 (US National Archives/
Roger-Viollet), 29 and 39 (Scherl/SV-Bilderdienst); iStockphoto: 44 (Tim Fan);
U.S. Air Force photo: 45.

LIBRARY OF CONGRESS CATALOGING–IN–PUBLICATION DATA
Souter, Gerry.
 Herbert Hoover / by Gerry and Janet Souter.
   p. cm. — (Presidents of the U.S.A.)
 Includes bibliographical references and index.
 ISBN 978–1–60253–059–1 (library bound : alk. paper)
 1. Hoover, Herbert, 1874–1964—Juvenile literature. 2. Presidents—United
States—Biography—Juvenile literature. I. Souter, Janet, 1940– II. Title.

E802.S69 2008
973.91'6092—dc22
[B]
                          2007049068

Herbert Hoover served as president from 1929 to 1933.

TABLE OF CONTENTS

A RELIGIOUS CHILDHOOD

Herbert Clark Hoover was born on August 10, 1874, in the small town of West Branch, Iowa. The town had a newspaper, a blacksmith shop, and a house where religious meetings were held. People worked hard in West Branch, and this work ethic became a strong influence on Herbert as he grew older.

Herbert, the cheerful second son of Jesse and Hulda Hoover, was nicknamed Bertie. His brother, Theodore, who was known as Tad, was three years older. In 1876, their sister, Mary, was born.

Religion was important to Bertie's family. There were prayer meetings in the Hoover home, and the family went to church meetings in town twice a week. This gave young Herbert "strong training in patience," he later remembered.

Hoover's mother, Hulda Minthorn Hoover, was a schoolteacher when she met Jesse Hoover.

Herbert Hoover (left) poses with his older brother, Theodore. Theodore grew up to become the head of the Stanford School of Engineering.

Herbert's father was a blacksmith. He made and repaired horseshoes and other iron goods. In 1878, he began manufacturing farm equipment. The business was successful. Sadly, Jesse soon became ill. He died in 1880 at the age of 34. Hulda did her best to keep the family together. She took in sewing and rented out a room in their house to make money.

After Jesse's death, religion became even more important to the Hoover family. The Hoovers belonged to the Quaker faith, which is a Christian **denomination.** Quakers have a deep belief in hard work and honesty. Both men and women can be leaders in the church. In 1883, Herbert's mother became a minister. She traveled throughout Iowa, preaching and holding prayer meetings. Relatives cared for the Hoover children while she was away.

Tragedy struck the Hoover family again in 1884, when Hulda died. The children were separated and sent to live with relatives. Herbert lived with his uncle

At the age of five, young Bertie Hoover loved conducting experiments. One day, his father left a bucket of tar outside his blacksmith shop. Bertie threw a flaming stick into the bucket to see what would happen. The tar instantly caught fire. People hurried with buckets of water to put out the flames. No one knows if Jesse Hoover ever found out his son had started the fire, but the event did make the local paper.

Allan. Herbert's older brother, Tad, stayed with another uncle, while Hulda's mother raised their sister, Mary. For a year and a half, Herbert enjoyed farm life with his uncle's family.

In November 1885, another uncle, Doctor John Minthorn, asked that Herbert come live with him in Oregon. His own son had recently died. With only a few coins in his pocket and some food prepared by his aunt, Herbert boarded a train for Newberg, Oregon.

John Minthorn ran a strict household. He insisted that young Herbert milk cows, gather firewood, and feed and water the horses. But he also wanted his nephew to have a good education. He sent Herbert to the Friends Pacific Academy in Newberg. Herbert was an average student in most subjects, but he did very well in mathematics. His uncle had a large library in his home, and Herbert read as much as possible. On Sundays, Herbert went to Quaker meetings, Sunday school, and Quaker youth gatherings. He also studied the Bible. On other days, Herbert went with Dr. Minthorn on long trips to visit patients. This added to his education, as he learned about the parts of the body and how they worked.

When Herbert was 14 years old, the family moved to the town of Salem, Oregon. His uncle opened a real estate office, called the Oregon Land Company, and Herbert worked there for two years.

John Minthorn was so busy selling real estate that he was seldom in the office. Herbert learned as much as he could about the business. When someone at the

Hoover had a scar on the bottom of his foot throughout his life. He got it as a child when he walked into his father's blacksmith shop barefoot and stepped on a glowing ember.

Quakers do not believe in using guns, so the Hoover boys learned to hunt with bows and arrows instead.

office had a question, Herbert always had the answer. He was also interested in other businesses. He and a friend repaired sewing machines and tried to sell them for a dollar. Nobody bought them. But if Herbert was unsuccessful in one venture, he tried another. He learned how to do bookkeeping and typing. He also helped advertise properties for sale by the Oregon Land Company.

While working in his uncle's office, Herbert met many different types of people. One man worked as an engineer. He made his living by designing new and better ways to do things. Herbert often spoke to the engineer and was curious about his work. A woman in the neighborhood convinced Herbert to take business classes at a nearby school.

Herbert Hoover was born in this tiny two-room house in West Branch, Iowa.

Hoover was a member of Stanford University's first graduating class. He is shown here seated at left with other engineering students.

The Oregon State Fair is held in Salem each year. While still a teenager, Herbert managed all the transportation for taking crowds of people to the fairgrounds.

When he was 17, Herbert decided he would study engineering at college. Stanford University in northern California had just opened and was looking for students. Herbert took the entrance exam that determined whether he would be admitted to the school. Though he was weak in other subjects, he did very well in math and was accepted. It looked as if he had the talent to become an engineer.

THE QUAKER WAY OF LIFE

The Quaker faith influenced Herbert Hoover's actions throughout his life. The Quakers' formal name is the Religious Society of Friends. They often call themselves simply "the Friends." For Quakers, living their faith means striving for peace and helping people who are less fortunate, especially those who are victims of an unjust law or way of life. The Friends are great believers in education and have a keen interest in world affairs. They believe their mission is to make the world a better place to live. Friends must strive throughout their lives to be good and decent.

The Friends believe that a person, no matter how poor, should find some way to earn a living rather than depend on the charity of others. Hoover remembered this philosophy all his life. He did what he could to help people, but he expected them to help themselves as well. An admirer of Hoover once said that if a man asked the president for a dime, he would not give it to him, but he would put him in touch with an agency that could find him work. The picture below shows Herbert and Lou Hoover leaving the Friends Meeting House in Washington, D.C., during his presidency.

CHAPTER TWO

ENGINEER AND WORLD TRAVELER

Herbert Hoover was a member of the first class at Stanford. His tuition was free, but he still had to work to pay for his textbooks, room, and food. To pay his expenses, he got a job as a clerk in the school's office. He also set up a student laundry service, and he became an assistant to the geology professor. Geology is the study of the earth's rocks and minerals. The subject fascinated him, and he decided to become a mining engineer.

Herbert Hoover quickly became wealthy working as a mining engineer. This photograph of him is from 1899.

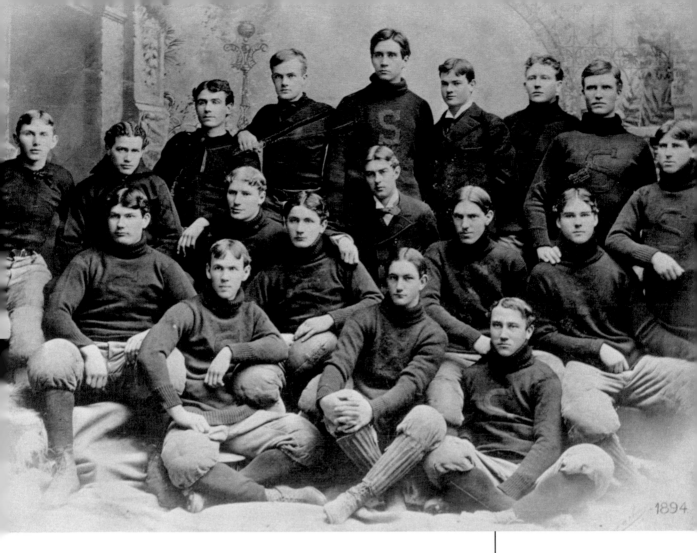

1894

Hoover stayed very busy at Stanford. In addition to his classwork and jobs, he also established the school's geology club, organized the school store, served as class treasurer, and managed the school's baseball team.

A woman named Lou Henry was also studying engineering at Stanford. She and Hoover had a lot in common. They had been born within 100 miles of each other in Iowa. They were both geology majors, and they both loved to fish. Herbert and Lou fell in love during Herbert's final year at Stanford. They made plans to marry as soon as he was able to support her.

Herbert Hoover (back row, fourth from right) poses with the Stanford football team. One of Hoover's many activities at Stanford was managing the team.

11

English was Herbert's most difficult subject at Stanford. He was told he could not graduate unless his writing was perfect. Every word had to be spelled correctly, and he could make no errors in grammar. His final paper was perfect and he was allowed to graduate.

After graduating from Stanford in 1895, Hoover worked nights in a California gold mine. It was back-breaking work, but it helped him to better understand his profession. Working in the mine taught him things he never could have learned from a book. Later, Hoover found a job in the office of a mining engineering company in San Francisco. His hard work eventually led to a job with Bewick, Moreing and Company, a British engineering firm.

The company sent the 22-year-old Hoover to Australia. He spent long hours in 100-degree weather, inspecting mines and searching for gold. He excelled at his work and helped the company earn a lot of money.

Hoover is shown here during his time in Australia. His job was to try to determine the value of mines in the region.

Lou Henry and Herbert Hoover pose with members of Lou's family on their wedding day in 1899. They left for China that very day.

Hoover himself earned $12,500 per year. Although that was a great deal of money at the time, it did not make him happy. Hoover was lonely. "Anyone who envies me my **salary** can . . . take my next trip with me," he once said. "He would be contented to be a bank clerk." Herbert longed to return home. He called the town in Australia where he lived "a place of red dust, black flies, and white heat . . . one of the hottest, driest, and dustiest places on this Earth."

Hoover returned to the United States in 1899 with one purpose—to marry Lou Henry. By then, she also had graduated from Stanford with a degree in geology. The day they were married, they left for Tianjin, a city in China where Hoover would work as a mining engineer.

Hoover didn't like Australia. It was hot and dusty, and whirlwinds called "willie willies" could rise up out of nowhere. They were fierce enough to carry away small shacks in clouds of dust.

AN UNCOMMON FIRST LADY

At the time Lou Henry graduated from Stanford University, most women in the United States didn't finish high school, much less go to college. Lou Henry was not like most women of her time. Before she was born, her father had dreamed of all the things he could do if he had a son. When his wife had a baby girl, he decided they could still have fun together. He took Lou with him to do all the things he enjoyed. He taught Lou all about nature and the outdoors. They fished, took hunting trips, and went camping, even though it was more common in those days for boys to enjoy these pastimes. Lou was also an excellent athlete. When people called her a tomboy, she didn't mind one bit.

After she married Herbert, Lou Hoover traveled all over the world with him. In fact, they departed for China on the very afternoon of their wedding. She was always ready for an adventure. In the picture above, she is looking at a gun used during the Boxer Rebellion.

As first lady, Lou Hoover was known for her kind treatment of the servants and staff who worked at the White House. When employees were ill, she had food sent to them from the White House kitchen. She saw to it that a White House butler was given proper medical treatment when he had tuberculosis, a serious disease of the lungs.

Lou Hoover believed that all people should be treated equally. She was as polite to Girl Scouts who visited the White House as she was to important politicians. Once, she invited Jessie Williams De Priest to tea at the White House. Mrs. De Priest was an the wife of Oscar De Priest, the first African American congressman elected from a northern state. At the time, some people still believed that African Americans should not be guests at the White House. That day, some guests refused to shake hands with Mrs. De Priest. But Lou did everything she could to make her feel at ease. In the photo below, Lou Hoover is shown signing cards for Girl Scouts.

The Boxers wanted to rid China of all foreign influence. This picture shows rebels destroying a telegraph line.

Lou Hoover sent letters home from China asking for clothing that they couldn't buy in Tianjin. She also asked for books and magazines because she and her husband loved to read.

At this time, foreigners controlled large parts of several port cities in China, including Tianjin. This enraged some Chinese, who felt that the foreigners had too much power in their country. They also worried that Westerners would spread Christianity across China, destroying their traditional religions. A group of **rebels** known as the Boxers emerged. They wanted to rid China of foreign influence.

The rebels moved across the countryside, burning churches and killing Christians. By June 1900, the Boxers neared Tianjin. Several foreign powers had sent troops to try to put down the Boxer Rebellion. Now many of these troops took refuge in Tianjin. The Chinese government also sent soldiers to help defend the city, but many of these soldiers refused to fight. Some even joined the Boxers. When the Boxers began bombarding the city, Hoover worked to defend it. He organized work parties to build **barricades,** using grain sacks from the city's warehouses. The people trapped in Tianjin fought 30,000 Boxers for nearly a month. Despite all the bombing and shooting, Hoover risked his life at night, sneaking out to get water for the people trapped behind the barricades. The Hoovers could not escape Tianjin until August. Finally, they were able to get onto a German mail boat headed for England.

After the Boxer Rebellion ended, the Hoovers returned to China for a time. But soon, Hoover's work took him to other parts of the world. The Hoovers' first child was born in London on August 4, 1903. They named him Herbert Clark Jr. For the next few years, the Hoovers brought their young son along on their travels. In 1907, they welcomed their second son, Allan Henry. The following year, Hoover left Bewick, Moreing and Company and returned to the United States. Lou Hoover wanted to raise their children at home.

Hoover formed his own engineering company in 1908. He soon became known as "the Great Engineer."

One day during the Boxer Rebellion, Lou Hoover was riding her bike around Tianjin when bullets hit the tires.

A New York newspaper reported that the Hoovers died during the Boxer Rebellion. Their family members were relieved to learn that this was not true.

17

Between 1902 and 1907, Herbert Hoover and his family traveled the globe five times.

During a trip to Southeast Asia, Hoover and another man were investigating an abandoned mine when they discovered a tiger living in one of the tunnels. "The tiger, fortunately . . . did not come out to greet us," he later wrote.

His company had offices in several cities, including London, New York, and San Francisco.

Hoover started his company because he had his own ideas about how an engineer should solve problems. He believed that first the engineer should consider whether the problem is worth solving. If it is, then the engineer should study the problem to decide how to handle it. The next step is to make plans to solve the problem. Only then would he begin work on the problem. This was an unusual way of thinking in the early 1900s. But this is how Herbert Hoover solved problems all his life, including the years he served in government.

Lou Henry with her sons Allan and Herbert Jr. The young family traveled constantly in the early 1900s.

CHAPTER THREE

THE HUMANITARIAN

By 1914, Hoover was worth nearly $10 million. He had so much money that he felt he should spend more time helping the less fortunate. He thought he should go into public service. In June 1914, World War I began when the countries of Germany and Austria-Hungary went to war against Great Britain, France, and Russia. Hoover was working in England at the time. Americans who were stranded in London were not able to get cash because the banks were closed. Hotels and shops wouldn't accept U.S. dollars or travelers checks from Americans. American officials asked Hoover for help. He took gold and British money from his offices and exchanged it for the Americans' funds. Hoover raised more than a million dollars to help the 120,000 American citizens in England. He soon became known as a **humanitarian** because of his dedication to helping others.

Hoover lived in London during much of the early 1900s, and he began his large-scale humanitarian work there.

Hoover also heard about the terrible conditions in the tiny nation of Belgium, which had been taken over by Germany. Belgium did not have much farmland, and its citizens depended on other nations to supply their food. But Germany refused to supply food for the Belgians. People were starving, and Hoover knew he had to do something. But how could he gather enough food to supply more than 10 million people every day? And how would he get the food to Belgium?

Hoover went to the war-torn country and formed a group called the Commission for Relief in Belgium. He raised money for food and arranged for transportation to take it to the people who needed it. Many problems arose, but Hoover handled them well. He did such a good job that when the United States entered the war in 1917, he was asked to take on a similar role for his own country.

The city of Ypres, Belgium, was almost completely destroyed during World War I.

Hoover first came to the attention of the American people for his work as a humanitarian. His efforts saved millions of people in Europe from starvation.

Hoover returned to the United States in 1917 to form the U.S. Food Administration. It was responsible for supplying food to American soldiers and to their **allies,** the soldiers of Great Britain and France. The U.S. Food Administration also had to make sure **civilians** in the United States, England, and France had enough food.

This was a difficult job, but Hoover never took any pay for it. He directed the operation with great care. He set up a food **conservation** plan, which included a system for storing wheat when it was plentiful and releasing it when it was scarce. An important part of Hoover's plan involved Americans conserving food at home. If people did not waste food, extra supplies could

21

During World War I, the U.S. Food Administration produced posters that urged Americans to conserve food. If Americans ate less, there would be more food to feed soldiers and others in Europe.

be sent to help soldiers and others overseas. The U.S. Food Administration asked Americans to make sacrifices and save food. Posters and signs told Americans that "Food Will Win the War" and "When in Doubt, Serve Potatoes." Americans were asked to have "meatless Mondays" and "wheatless Wednesdays." This type of conservation became known as "Hooverizing." Hoover wanted people to conserve voluntarily, and people cooperated, both in the United States and in Europe. Hoover didn't believe that the government should tell people what to do. He felt that a **democracy** depended on the strength of each citizen. This belief stayed with him all his life.

Hoover's job of feeding the hungry did not end once the war was over in 1918. The Commission for Relief in Belgium and the U.S. Food Administration worked together to help America's allies as well as its former enemies, the Germans. Germany faced terrible problems at the end of World War I. President Woodrow Wilson asked Hoover to help Germans and other Europeans begin growing crops. People criticized Hoover for helping the enemy. But he felt that people—especially children—should not be left to starve. "Twenty million people are starving," he said, "whatever their **politics** they should be fed." He asked the Friends Service Committee, a Quaker organization, to lead separate operations for Germany. After the war, Hoover led the American Relief Administration, which fed 350 million people in 21 countries.

Millions of people in Europe were starving in the aftermath of World War I. This picture shows children in Germany lining up for a free meal.

FEEDING THE WORLD

In November 1918, President Woodrow Wilson put Herbert Hoover in charge of helping feed the starving people in post-war Europe. Hoover knew the people needed nourishing food to rebuild their nations. In fact, he asked President Wilson for the job, because he felt confident he was the best person to accomplish this difficult task.

Hoover established operation headquarters in Paris, France. He began by taking charge of railroads, river transportation, and communications. He also restarted coal production to keep homes and factories warm. In addition, he provided medical care to control diseases that had run rampant during the war.

When Hoover returned home in 1919, he was proud of his accomplishments. His organization had supplied more than 20 nations with food, clothing, seeds for planting, and other supplies. His caring nature and his skills had fed millions of people around the world.

Hoover's work in Europe was finished in 1919, and he gladly returned home. He was now so well known that people from both of the major **political parties,** the Democrats and the Republicans, thought he should run for president. But Hoover wanted a quiet life. He and Lou built a home in California near Stanford University. Lou designed their house herself. The family prepared to settle into a quiet life at home.

Hoover didn't remain idle for long, however. Between 1919 and 1921, he made 46 speeches and wrote more than 50 magazine articles. He also led conferences and spoke before Congress.

Warren Harding was elected president in 1920. He named Hoover the secretary of **commerce.** In this position, Hoover advised the president on business matters. At the time, this was not considered a time-consuming position. It took only a few hours a day. But Hoover was not content playing such a small role. He expanded the agency and made it a vital part of the

Workers at the Commission for Relief in Belgium knew that growing children needed a healthy diet to protect them from disease. They created a special cookie that contained all the essential foods a child's body needs. They served it with milk and stew to more than 2.5 million children.

Lou Hoover designed the Hoovers' home in Palo Alto, California.

In 1921, Hoover was offered a partnership with the largest mining company in the world. His salary would increase by a half million dollars each year. At the same time, he was also offered the job as secretary of commerce, which paid much less. Hoover felt he could do more good for more people as secretary of commerce, so he took that job.

Lou Hoover devoted much of her time to the Girl Scouts of America. She wanted young girls to love the outdoors. She went on hikes with the Girl Scouts, visited their camps, and took part in many of their events. She was both a troop leader and a member of the Girl Scout Council in Washington, D.C.

government. Under Hoover's direction, the Commerce Department began to offer more advice and information to help businesses around the country. Hoover took steps to increase regulations in order to make workplaces safer. He also encouraged businesses to make their products in uniform sizes. If the companies that produced goods such as light bulbs, paper, or nuts and bolts made them in the same size, parts from different companies could be used together.

While secretary of commerce, Hoover led the way in making **technology** a driving force in the United States. **Aviation** was a new and exciting field. Hoover thought that airplanes could be used to deliver mail more quickly. He encouraged airport crews to install lights on runways to make takeoffs and landings safer. Television was also being developed during the 1920s. The first public demonstration of television featured Herbert Hoover.

As secretary of commerce, Hoover found ways to lower the **unemployment** rate. He worked with leaders in banking, construction, agriculture, and labor. Together they developed construction projects. Soon companies began hiring more workers. When companies had problems between management and labor, Hoover stepped in and helped settle the disputes.

Hoover also got involved in many other aspects of American business and life. He showed businesses how to use water carefully, so there was no waste. He wrote a booklet, "How to Own Your Own Home." It sold millions of copies. He helped architects design more

As secretary of commerce, Herbert Hoover participated in the first demonstration of a television broadcast between two cities.

efficient homes. He also worked with charitable groups to study food problems. Children's health remained an important issue for Hoover. He wanted all American children to get **vaccinations** against disease. He also encouraged the government to provide milk and hot lunches to poor children.

The 1920s was a time of growth and **prosperity.** Many industries reduced the workday to eight hours, giving people more time off. Because wages were high and the **economy** was strong, lots of people purchased goods on a "payment plan." This meant that they bought goods and paid for them a little at a time, a system similar to the credit cards people use today. Everyone thought the good times would go on forever. But hard times were just around the corner.

Herbert Hoover was a wealthy man for most of his adult life. He took no pay for his humanitarian work during World War I. He also refused to be paid for serving as president. He donated his presidential salary to charity.

CHAPTER FOUR

A TROUBLED PRESIDENCY

Herbert Hoover had stayed on as secretary of commerce under President Calvin Coolidge. In 1928, when Coolidge decided not to run for reelection, Hoover's friends began a "Hoover for President" campaign. His political enemies in the Republican Party were jealous of his popularity, but they knew that Hoover had the best chance of winning the presidency. Hoover was chosen as the Republican **candidate.** His opponent was Alfred Smith, a member of the Democratic Party. The nation had enjoyed success with the last two Republican presidents. People had confidence in their leadership, and Hoover easily won the election.

Herbert Hoover's **inauguration** took place on March 4, 1929. For the first time ever, Americans could hear the ceremony on the radio. Hoover's early days in office promised good times and

Herbert Hoover was elected president in 1928.

a bright future. President Hoover started many major building projects, including the Hoover Dam near Las Vegas, Nevada, and the Grand Coulee Dam in the state of Washington. He added five million acres of land to the national forest and park systems. This land was set aside for recreation and to conserve the wilderness areas.

Hoover reduced taxes for families with low **incomes.** Because farmers around the country were having a difficult time earning a living, Hoover created the Federal Farm Board. The board worked to sell more produce to other countries. It also helped farmers earn more money for their crops by raising prices.

Construction began on the massive Hoover Dam in 1931. It took five years to complete.

Hoover believed that children were America's hope for the future. "If we could have but one generation of properly born, trained, educated and healthy children, a thousand other problems of government would vanish," he once said.

In 1932, Hoover ran for president against Franklin D. Roosevelt. Twelve years earlier, Roosevelt had said that he hoped Hoover would be president some day. "There could not be a better one," Roosevelt said.

Less than a year after Hoover entered office, the good times ended. October 29, 1929, is known as "Black Friday." It is the day the **stock market** crashed. The value of a company is largely based on the price people are willing to pay for its stock, which are shares of the company. When stock is sold cheaply, the company is considered to be worth less than when prices are high.

Many **investors** in the 1920s bought stock with money they had borrowed from banks. They hoped that stock prices would rise. If that happened, they would make a **profit.** From that profit, investors planned to pay back the money they had borrowed. For a few years, this worked. But at the end of the decade, many companies began to lose money. This lowered the price of stock. Investors did not make the profits they hoped they would. Because of this they could not repay the money they had borrowed. Many banks went out of business when investors couldn't repay their loans. People who had savings in these banks lost their money as well.

Companies lost money when stock prices fell. They had to fire many employees. People without jobs could not afford to buy the products companies made, causing businesses to lose even more money. This difficult period in history is known as the Great Depression.

At first, people thought that the Depression would last a short time. Hoover dealt with the Depression the same way as he dealt with any other problem. He studied the problem and came up with solutions he thought would work. The government encouraged people to spend money and buy products to boost the economy. For a few months, it worked. But unemployment continued to rise. Hoover established the President's Committee for Unemployment Relief. These were local groups set up to help feed the hungry. He wanted people to think that the bad times were nearly over. But there was little change, and Americans stopped believing in Hoover's ability to solve this problem.

Times were tough for the rest of Hoover's presidency. Each year, farmers received less money for their crops. Even the Federal Farm Board was unable to help. Banks had very little money. No matter what ideas Hoover came up with, he had little support from Congress or from American businesses.

President Hoover signed an act that made "The Star-Spangled Banner" the U.S. national anthem.

Many banks went out of business during the Great Depression. Here, an angry crowd eager to get their money back gathers in front of a bank that has closed.

Construction began on the Hoover Dam in Nevada while Hoover was president. The dam wasn't completed until Franklin D. Roosevelt's presidency. Roosevelt renamed it Boulder Dam because Hoover had been so unpopular during his presidency. President Harry Truman changed the name back to Hoover Dam in 1947.

In 1932, Hoover created the Reconstruction Finance Corporation (RFC). Its purpose was to loan money to businesses that were vital to the nation's economy. The RFC also loaned money to state and local governments. Unfortunately, this did little to help the economy. Still, Hoover believed that people should not expect the government to give them money. "I am confident that our people have the resources . . . to meet this situation in the way they have met their problems over generations." He meant that Americans had always had the ability to solve their own problems without help from the government. He did not believe that should change, even in such a severe crisis as the Depression. This attitude made people angry. Many people without jobs had to live in cardboard shacks. Settlements of these shacks grew up in many cities. People called them Hoovervilles.

With no jobs or savings, people went hungry during the Great Depression. Many people went to soup kitchens to get a free meal.

Although Hoover still believed that the Great Depression would soon be over, things only grew worse. In his last year in office, he began new government programs to provide for hungry Americans. He also tried to help banks. But most Americans thought Hoover hadn't done enough—and that he had waited too long to do what little he did.

Democrat Franklin D. Roosevelt easily beat Hoover in the presidential election of 1932. Roosevelt's outgoing personality made Americans trust him. He promised to help people. Hoover felt that voters had judged him unfairly. "I had little hope of reelection in 1932," he wrote. "One of Roosevelt's most effective campaign issues was to allege that I had made the Depression and then done nothing about it."

The Depression left many people homeless. Desperate people built shacks using whatever materials they could find.

Hoover loved fishing. After leaving the presidency, he escaped with his fishing pole whenever he could.

Hoover liked getting letters from children, and he always answered them. In 1962, he put his letters to children in a book titled *On Growing Up*.

After President Hoover left office, he and Lou returned to their California home. They later had an apartment in New York City as well. As the nation struggled with the Depression and then World War II, they led a quiet life. The Hoovers enjoyed fishing, reading, and spending time with their family. Then, in 1944, Lou Henry Hoover died suddenly of a heart attack.

President Roosevelt died the following year. His vice president, Harry Truman, became president. Truman remembered Hoover's talents and soon put them to use. World War II ended in 1945. The war had left much of Europe devastated. In 1946, Truman asked Hoover to help Europeans recover from the destruction.

Truman next asked Hoover to lead a committee to make the U.S. government work more smoothly and efficiently. This became known as the Hoover Commission. President Truman felt that the federal government had too many departments that cost too much money. Both Democrats and Republicans served on the Hoover Commission. They found ways to eliminate some departments, while combining others. They also created new departments, such as the Department of Health, Education and Welfare. The commission suggested 273 changes in the government. Congress accepted about 70 percent of the suggestions. This saved the taxpayers several billion dollars. Many states followed this example. They established what were known as Little Hoover Commissions. Hoover led a second Hoover Commission in the 1950s. During this time, Hoover also wrote several books.

Children lead Hoover through Warsaw, Poland, after World War II. In 1946, President Truman sent Hoover as a special representative to help Europe recover from the devastation of the war. Hoover's job was to study and help solve the food shortage, just as he had done after World War I.

By the early 1960s, Hoover's health was failing. He attended the opening of the Hoover Presidential Library and Museum in West Branch, Iowa, in 1962. But when he returned to New York, he became ill. Herbert Hoover died on October 20, 1964. He was 90 years old.

Hoover is most often remembered as the president who failed to rescue the nation from the Great Depression. But later in his life, people remembered all the good he had done. He worked hard to see that food was provided for both Americans and Europeans during wartime. He also promoted science and industry.

The Great Depression challenged all the nation's leaders. Perhaps Herbert Hoover could have been a great president in different times, for he loved his country and its people. "Within the soul of America is freedom of mind and spirit," he once said. "Perhaps it's not perfect, but it's more full of its realization than any other place in the world."

Herbert Hoover stayed active well into his 80s. In 1958, he published a book called The Ordeal of Woodrow Wilson, *which became a best-seller. It was the first time one former president had written a biography of another former president.*

THE BONUS ARMY

The U.S. Congress promised to give **veterans** of World War I a $1,000 bonus for their efforts, but they had to wait until 1945 to collect it. In 1932, the country was suffering from the Great Depression. The veterans needed their bonus money immediately to feed and clothe their families. Some veterans decided to go to Washington and demand their bonus money. They became known as the Bonus Army. The veterans in the picture above are on their way to Washington, D.C., from Georgia.

By June, more than 20,000 veterans had arrived in Washington. President Hoover knew that the government did not have the money to pay the former soldiers. He would not give in to the Bonus Army's demands, but he did provide them with blankets, food, and medical supplies.

The veterans camped out in Washington. After several weeks, their presence became a serious problem. They begged for food and asked strangers for money. Police tried to force them to leave, but they refused. A riot broke out, and Hoover asked General Douglas MacArthur to break it up.

The general gathered 800 soldiers. Hoover only wanted MacArthur's troops to send the rioters back to their campsites. But the troops threw tear-gas bombs to break up the mob. Hoover ordered MacArthur to leave the men alone. The general refused and sent his soldiers into the camp with orders to burn everything. After this, the veterans left. Hoover never told Americans that MacArthur disobeyed his orders. Perhaps he felt that, as president, he was responsible for what had happened.

Time Line

1874
Herbert Hoover is born in West Branch, Iowa, on August 10. He is the second son of Jesse and Hulda Hoover.

1880
Hoover's father dies.

1884
Hoover's mother dies. Hoover and his siblings are separated and sent to live with relatives.

1885
After living with his uncle Allan in West Branch, Hoover is sent to live with his uncle John Minthorn, in Newberg, Oregon. Herbert attends the Friends Pacific Academy in Newberg.

1888
Hoover moves with the Minthorn family to Salem, Oregon. John Minthorn opens a real estate office, and Hoover works for him.

1891
Hoover enters Stanford University, a new college in California. He begins studying to become a mining engineer.

1895
Hoover graduates from Stanford with a degree in geology.

1897
After working at several mining jobs in the West, Hoover is hired by Bewick, Moreing and Company, which sends him to Australia to oversee mining operations.

1899
Hoover marries Lou Henry, his college girlfriend. They immediately leave for Tianjin, China.

1900
Chinese rebels known as the Boxers revolt against their government. They want to eliminate all foreign influences from their country. Lou and Herbert Hoover are trapped in Tianjin during the conflict, which is called the Boxer Rebellion.

1901
The Hoovers move to London, England. Herbert Hoover is made a partner at Bewick, Moreing and Company.

1903
The Hoovers' first child, Herbert Clark Jr., is born in London.

1907
The Hoovers' second child, Allan Henry, is born.

1908
Hoover leaves Bewick, Moreing and Company to open his own engineering firm.

1914
World War I begins. Hoover is asked to help raise money for Americans stranded in London who are trying to return to the United States. He also sets up food supply operations for Belgium's war victims.

1917
The United States enters World War I. President Woodrow Wilson asks Hoover to head the U.S. Food Administration.

1918
World War I ends.

1919
Hoover leads the American Relief Administration. It feeds the starving people in postwar Europe. The organization feeds 350 million people in 21 countries.

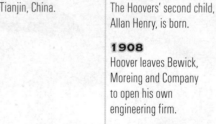

1920
President Warren Harding names Hoover the secretary of commerce. Hoover remains in this position for eight years.

1927
Hoover is pictured on the first demonstration of television signals.

1928
Hoover wins the presidential election, defeating New York governor Alfred Smith.

1929
Hoover is inaugurated on March 4. He starts many building projects and adds millions of acres to the nation's national forests and parks. He also reduces taxes for people with low incomes and creates the Federal Farm Board to help farmers. The stock market crashes on October 29, and the Great Depression begins. Millions of Americans lose their jobs and homes.

1932
The Bonus Army marches on Washington. Hoover is criticized when General Douglas MacArthur breaks up the protest, although MacArthur acted without the president's orders. Franklin D. Roosevelt defeats Hoover in the presidential election.

1933
Herbert and Lou return to their home in California.

1934
The Hoovers take an apartment in New York at the Waldorf Astoria Hotel.

1944
Lou Henry Hoover dies on January 7 in their New York apartment.

1945
President Roosevelt dies. Vice President Harry Truman is sworn in as president.

1946
President Harry Truman names Hoover the head of the war relief effort at the end of World War II.

1947
Hoover is appointed to head the Hoover Commission to make government more efficient.

1953
President Dwight D. Eisenhower appoints Hoover to chair the second Hoover Commission to reorganize the government.

1962
The Hoover Presidential Library and Museum opens in West Branch, Iowa, on August 10, Hoover's 88th birthday.

1964
Herbert Hoover dies on October 20 in New York.

GLOSSARY

allies (AL-lize) Allies are nations that have agreed to help each other by fighting together against a common enemy. The U.S. Food Administration was responsible for supplying food to U.S. allies in World War I.

aviation (ay-vee-AY-shun) Aviation is the science of flying airplanes. Aviation was a new field when Hoover was the secretary of commerce.

barricades (BAYR-uh-kaydz) Barricades are walls or fences built quickly to stop an enemy. During the Boxer Rebellion, Hoover built barricades out of grain sacks.

candidate (KAN-duh-dayt) A candidate is a person running in an election. Alfred Smith was the Democratic candidate in the 1928 presidential election.

civilians (suh-VIL-yunz) Civilians are people who are not in the military. During World War I, Hoover worked to make sure that American civilians had enough food.

commerce (KOM-urss) Commerce is the buying and selling of goods. Hoover was the secretary of commerce in the 1920s, a job that put him in charge of the nation's business affairs.

conservation (kon-sur-VAY-shun) Conservation is the act of using something carefully so that it does not run out. Hoover set up a conservation plan to make sure there would not be a shortage of food during World War I.

democracy (di-MAW-kreh-see) A democracy is a country in which the government is run by the people who live there. The United States is a democracy.

denomination (di-nah-muh-NAY-shun) A denomination is a religious organization whose members agree on certain beliefs. The Hoovers were Quakers, a Christian denomination.

economy (ee-KON-uh-mee) An economy is the way money is earned and spent in a country. In the 1920s, the economy was strong, and American companies made a lot of money.

humanitarian (hyoo-man-uh-TAYR-ee-un) A humanitarian is a person who cares for the welfare of others. Hoover was a humanitarian.

inauguration (ih-nawg-yuh-RAY-shun) An inauguration is the ceremony that takes place when a new president begins a term. Hoover's inauguration took place on March 4, 1929.

incomes (IN-kumz) People's incomes are the amounts of money that they earn. Hoover lowered taxes for people with low incomes.

investors (in-VES-turz) Investors are people who use money to buy something that they hope will make a profit, such as stock. Investors in the stock market lost money during the Great Depression.

political parties (puh-LIT-uh-kul PAR-teez) Political parties are groups of people who share similar ideas about how to run a government. Hoover belonged to the Republican political party.

politics (PAWL-uh-tiks) Politics refers to the actions and practices of the government. Politics can also be peoples' opinions about how a government should be run. Hoover said the United States should help starving people in Germany after World War I, even if their politics were different from his.

profit (PRAW-fut) Profit is money gained from a business or an investment. People who put their money into the stock market in the 1920s hoped to make a profit.

prosperity (pros-PAYR-uh-tee) Prosperity is success or good fortune. The 1920s was a time of prosperity in the United States.

rebels (REB-ulz) Rebels are people who fight against their government or other people in power. The Boxers were a group of rebels in China.

salary (SAL-uh-ree) A salary is money a person is paid regularly for work. As an engineer, Hoover earned a high salary.

stock market (STOK MAR-kit) The stock market is where people buy and sell small pieces of ownership in different companies. These pieces are called "shares" or "stock." Companies share their profits with people who own their stock.

technology (tek-NAWL-uh-jee) Technology is the use of scientific knowledge to create things that improve people's lives, such as telephones or computers. Aviation was a new form of technology when Hoover was the secretary of commerce.

unemployment (un-im-PLOY-munt) Unemployment is the state of not having a job. Unemployment rose during the Great Depression.

vaccinations (vak-suh-NAY-shunz) Vaccinations are shots or medications that protect people from disease. Hoover wanted young children to receive vaccinations.

veterans (VE-tuh-runz) Veterans are people who have served in the military, especially during a war. Veterans of World War I were promised bonus money for fighting in the war.

THE UNITED STATES GOVERNMENT

The United States government is divided into three equal branches: the executive, the legislative, and the judicial. This division helps prevent abuses of power because each branch has to answer to the other two. No one branch can become too powerful.

EXECUTIVE BRANCH

PRESIDENT
VICE PRESIDENT
DEPARTMENTS

The job of the executive branch is to enforce the laws. It is headed by the president, who serves as the spokesperson for the United States around the world. The president signs bills into law and appoints important officials such as federal judges. He or she is also the commander in chief of the U.S. military. The president is assisted by the vice president, who takes over if the president dies or cannot carry out the duties of the office.

The executive branch also includes various departments, each focused on a specific topic. They include the Defense Department, the Justice Department, and the Agriculture Department. The department heads, along with other officials such as the vice president, serve as the president's closest advisers, called the cabinet.

LEGISLATIVE BRANCH

CONGRESS
Senate and
House of Representatives

The job of the legislative branch is to make the laws. It consists of Congress, which is divided into two parts: the Senate and the House of Representatives. The Senate has 100 members, and the House of Representatives has 435 members. Each state has two senators. The number of representatives a state has varies depending on the state's population.

Besides making laws, Congress also passes budgets and enacts taxes. In addition, it is responsible for declaring war, maintaining the military, and regulating trade with other countries.

JUDICIAL BRANCH

SUPREME COURT
COURTS OF APPEALS
DISTRICT COURTS

The job of the judicial branch is to interpret the laws. It consists of the nation's federal courts. Trials are held in district courts. During trials, judges must decide what laws mean and how they apply. Courts of appeals review the decisions made in district courts.

The nation's highest court is the Supreme Court. If someone disagrees with a court of appeals ruling, he or she can ask the Supreme Court to review it. The Supreme Court may refuse. The Supreme Court makes sure that decisions and laws do not violate the Constitution.

CHOOSING
THE PRESIDENT

It may seem odd, but American voters don't elect the president directly. Instead, the president is chosen using what is called the Electoral College.

Each state gets as many votes in the Electoral College as its combined total of senators and representatives in Congress. For example, Iowa has two senators and five representatives, so it gets seven electoral votes. Although the District of Columbia does not have any voting members in Congress, it gets three electoral votes. Usually, the candidate who wins the most votes in any given state receives all of that state's electoral votes.

To become president, a candidate must get more than half of the Electoral College votes. There are a total of 538 votes in the Electoral College, so a candidate needs 270 votes to win. If nobody receives 270 Electoral College votes, the House of Representatives chooses the president.

With the Electoral College system, the person who receives the most votes nationwide does not always receive the most electoral votes. This happened most recently in 2000, when Al Gore received half a million more national votes than George W. Bush. Bush became president because he had more Electoral College votes.

THE WHITE HOUSE

The White House is the official home of the president of the United States. It is located at 1600 Pennsylvania Avenue NW in Washington, D.C. In 1792, a contest was held to select the architect who would design the president's home. James Hoban won. Construction took eight years.

The first president, George Washington, never lived in the White House. The second president, John Adams, moved into the house in 1800, though the inside was not yet complete. During the War of 1812, British soldiers burned down much of the White House. It was rebuilt several years later.

The White House was changed through the years. Porches were added, and President Theodore Roosevelt added the West Wing. President William Taft changed the shape of the presidential office, making it into the famous Oval Office. While Harry Truman was president, the old house was discovered to be structurally weak. All the walls were reinforced with steel, and the rooms were rebuilt.

Today, the White House has 132 rooms (including 35 bathrooms), 28 fireplaces, and 3 elevators. It takes 570 gallons of paint to cover the outside of the six-story building. The White House provides the president with many ways to relax. It includes a putting green, a jogging track, a swimming pool, a tennis court, and beautifully landscaped gardens. The White House also has a movie theater, a billiard room, and a one-lane bowling alley.

PRESIDENTIAL PERKS

The job of president of the United States is challenging. It is probably one of the most stressful jobs in the world. Because of this, presidents are paid well, though not nearly as well as the leaders of large corporations. In 2007, the president earned $400,000 a year. Presidents also receive extra benefits that make the demanding job a little more appealing.

★ **Camp David:** In the 1940s, President Franklin D. Roosevelt chose this heavily wooded spot in the mountains of Maryland to be the presidential retreat, where presidents can relax. Even though it is a retreat, world business is conducted there. Most famously, President Jimmy Carter met with Middle Eastern leaders at Camp David in 1978. The result was a peace agreement between Israel and Egypt.

★ *Air Force One*: The president flies on a jet called *Air Force One*. It is a Boeing 747-200B that has been modified to meet the president's needs.

Air Force One is the size of a large home. It is equipped with a dining room, sleeping quarters, a conference room, and office space. It also has two kitchens that can provide food for up to 50 people.

★ **The Secret Service:** While not the most glamorous of the president's perks, the Secret Service is one of the most important. The Secret Service is a group of highly trained agents who protect the president and the president's family.

★ **The Presidential State Car:** The presidential limousine is a stretch Cadillac DTS.

It has been armored to protect the president in case of attack. Inside the plush car are a foldaway desk, an entertainment center, and a communications console.

★ **The Food:** The White House has five chefs who will make any food the president wants. The White House also has an extensive wine collection.

★ **Retirement:** A former president receives a pension, or retirement pay, of just under $180,000 a year. Former presidents also receive Secret Service protection for the rest of their lives.

FACTS

QUALIFICATIONS

To run for president, a candidate must

- ★ be at least 35 years old
- ★ be a citizen who was born in the United States
- ★ have lived in the United States for 14 years

TERM OF OFFICE

A president's term of office is four years.
No president can stay in office for more than two terms.

ELECTION DATE

The presidential election takes place every four years on the first Tuesday of November.

INAUGURATION DATE

Presidents are inaugurated on January 20.

OATH OF OFFICE

I do solemnly swear I will faithfully execute the office of the President of the United States and will to the best of my ability preserve, protect, and defend the Constitution of the United States.

WRITE A LETTER TO THE PRESIDENT

One of the best things about being a U.S. citizen is that Americans get to participate in their government. They can speak out if they feel government leaders aren't doing their jobs. They can also praise leaders who are going the extra mile. Do you have something you'd like the president to do? Should the president worry more about the environment and encourage people to recycle? Should the government spend more money on our schools? You can write a letter to the president to say how you feel!

1600 Pennsylvania Avenue
Washington, D.C. 20500
You can even send an e-mail to: president@whitehouse.gov

BOOKS

Burgan, Michael. *The Great Depression.* Minneapolis: Compass Point Books, 2002.

Colbert, Nancy A. *Lou Henry Hoover: The Duty to Serve.* Greensboro, NC: Morgan Reynolds, 1988.

Feinberg, Barbara Silberdick. *America's First Ladies.* New York: Franklin Watts, 1998.

Freedman, Russell. *Children of the Great Depression.* New York: Clarion Books, 2005.

Hilton, Suzanne. *The World of Young Herbert Hoover.* New York: Walker and Company, 1987.

Kendall, Martha E. *Herbert Hoover.* New York: Children's Press, 2004.

Landau, Elaine. *The Great Depression.* New York: Children's Press, 2006.

Teitelbaum, Michael. *Herbert Hoover.* Minneapolis: Compass Point Books, 2003.

Williams, Jean Kinney. *The Quakers.* New York: Franklin Watts, 1998.

VIDEOS

The History Channel Presents The Presidents. DVD (New York: A&E Home Video, 2005).

National Geographic's Inside the White House. DVD (Washington, DC: National Geographic Video, 2003).

INTERNET SITES

Visit our Web page for lots of links about Herbert Hoover and other U.S. presidents:

http://www.childsworld.com/links

Note to Parents, Teachers, and Librarians: We routinely verify our Web links to make sure they are safe, active sites—so encourage your readers to check them out!

INDEX